SOUTHERN STYLE
DECORATING

SOUTHERN STYLE
DECORATING

hm | books

Contents

INTRODUCTION 9

SECRETS TO SOUTHERN STYLE 10

TRADITION OF HOSPITALITY 17

SUBTLE & SOPHISTICATED 28

LIVING IN HARMONY 34

CLASSICAL RENDITION 42

CULTIVATED ELEGANCE 54

ARTISTIC IMPRESSION 64

FARMHOUSE HEART & SOUL 80

EVERYTHING IS ILLUMINATED 88

RUSTIC REDEFINED 100

THE COMFORTS OF HOME 112

ECLECTIC & EXQUISITE 122

THE COLOR OF WONDERFUL 130

NAUTICAL GETAWAY 142

LAKESIDE CHATEAU 152

LOWCOUNTRY GRANDEUR 162

SIGNATURE ITALIAN STYLE 172

PERSONAL COLLECTION 180

OUTDOOR INSPIRATION 190

HOME, SWEET HOME 198

ACKNOWLEDGMENTS 206

Introduction

Welcome to the South, where the spirit of hospitality flows from the front porch to the backyard patio. Our homes are more than dwelling places; they are personal retreats where memories are made. Throughout the halls and walls, we cultivate collections that reflect our personal styles and preferences, and in turn, these fabrics and furnishings help tell the stories of who we are and what we love. Southern style is as identifiable as the signature drawl associated with the region. Traditional, contemporary, rustic, casual, whimsical—the interpretations, much like dialects, are diverse, yet somehow the South's unmistakable spirit of hospitality punctuates each one. As we tour some of the most inviting and interesting spaces below the Mason-Dixon line, we will meet the people connected to the places and will discover expert tips on how to turn a house into a home. We hope each page will inspire and delight along the way, prompting fresh, creative ideas for projects of all shapes, sizes, and budgets. And remember: You can increase the beauty of any space simply by adding to the atmosphere kindness, grace, and joy.

secrets to
SOUTHERN STYLE

From thoughtful details to personal flourishes, the region's signature looks embrace heritage and elevate the art of hospitality. Learn how to translate these sensibilities into design and décor, and discover the divine appeal of a home saturated in Southern graces.

Inside and out, details make the difference. Punchy pillows dress up a porch swing, while window boxes add exponential curb appeal. It's not about doing big things, but, rather, small ones, with great love.

"If you love something, it will work. That's the only real rule."

— BUNNY WILLIAMS

Enrich your home with purposeful and sincere details. Potted ferns and flowers near the front door extend a warm welcome, and fresh-cut blooms add instant beauty all around the house. Look for foundational pieces—such as tile and countertops—that are high in quality as well as versatility, which will provide a classic canvas and allow plenty of scope for the imagination. Custom bed linens and draperies lend unparalleled personal charm, while monograms punctuate accent pieces with timeless appeal. Create depth in design by incorporating pieces with stories to tell—family heirlooms, interesting collections, and antique finds. Remember: Southern style is about making spaces livable, approachable, and inviting.

tradition of
HOSPITALITY

Allured by its historical charm, Connie and Rusty Stephenson purchased a Victorian home in Huntsville, Alabama, knowing it required an extensive remodel. Originally constructed in 1888, the structure had been subjected to a number of poorly executed additions by previous owners. To keep from repeating the mistakes of the past, they partnered with designer Beverly Farrington of Accents of the South, who began the project by consulting the home's original blueprints. "Though we were adding state-of-the-art appliances, lighting, and plumbing, our main goal was to enhance the original building style and design of the home," Beverly explains. From the gingerbread trim and lacy carved corbels on the front porch to the craftsman details included in the airy, open interiors, the finished renovation preserved the home's 19th-century character while also creating a comfortable living space for the family. "The Stephensons wanted the feeling of Southern graciousness," Beverly says of the pervading tone of the remodel. With an open-concept den and kitchen area at the heart of the home, well-appointed bedrooms throughout, and a showpiece rose garden outside, each facet was designed to put visitors and family alike elegantly at ease. "By using good aesthetic sense, we were able to create timeless interiors with modern sensibilities," the designer reflects.

"I believe homes are a reflection of our innermost self," says designer Beverly Farrington. For the Stephensons, that meant blending the beloved pieces they owned with newer items that fit the design plan. In the living room, a contemporary brass-and-glass coffee table complemented a classic Sheraton settee and tufted love seat. The collection created an updated look that remained true to the home's historical roots. To keep the rooms bright and open, Beverly used light greens and blues throughout, accenting them with buttery yellows, coral, and raspberry.

An antique chandelier and lovely damask draperies in the dining room reinforced the home's Victorian heritage, as did the glass transoms above the doorways. Adding natural light was integral to the renovation, and the Stephensons' addition included a windowed corridor that kept the stately interiors from feeling cramped.

Using soft fabrics and fine linens, Beverly designed each bedroom with comfort in mind. The dark wood tones in the furniture created an antique feel without seeming fussy, and special homage to the Victorian era came with the blue trellis-patterned wallpaper in one of the guest rooms. In the master suite, soft aqua walls set a tranquil tone underscored by luxurious bedding and generous window light.

The master's en suite bath included gleaming marble floors, along with a freestanding tub and a crystal chandelier. In each of the rooms, framed prints of impressionist paintings added interest without unsettling the calming tone of the cool interiors.

"I believe in creating homes that are the reflection of my client's personal sense of place—where great design, meaningful furnishings, color, and texture coax emotion as you walk over the threshold."

— BEVERLY FARRINGTON

High on homeowner Connie Stephenson's wish list was an expansive space where the family could cook, dine, and visit. With an open-concept kitchen attached to a comfortable den and dining area, her vision became a reality. Opening onto the patio, this cherished room is just steps from the Stephensons' beautifully cultivated garden.

The exquisite rose garden offers additional space for entertaining and relaxing. Beverly chose the furniture cushions' pink fabric to mimic the hues of the roses in bloom. A wonder to behold, the space includes lovely statuary and stone benches tucked among the fragrant flowers.

subtle &
SOPHISTICATED

When the Millers hired Dallas-based design firm A Well Dressed Home, the couple had one important request: "They wanted all the furnishings to be comfortable and livable, yet sophisticated," recall design consultants Emily Hewett and Allison Walker. From there, the Millers' open floor plan became a brilliant blank slate. "We knew these homeowners love to entertain, so we wanted to select furnishings and fabrics that would really make their guests feel welcome," Emily says. "We found our inspiration through listening to our clients' needs and desires for their space, and we were also inspired by a few items they had already purchased for their home." When it comes to the "big" pieces, such as seating and rugs, the team encouraged their clients to invest. "A good piece of furniture will provide more comfort and last so much longer," Emily says. "Staying neutral with the big pieces allows you to get creative with accessories and pillows, which can easily be changed out as your tastes change." For the Millers, a muted palette of creams, grays, and pale hues was punctuated by not-too-tame, not-too-trendy textures and patterns. From warm wood and animal prints to a classic Greek key trim along the bottom of the living-room-chair skirts, their home's sophisticated style proved to be anything but boring. Even in the office, style abounds, and the pristine finishes gave the entire home an identity that is fresh, contemporary, and absolutely lovely.

RIGHT: Although certainly stunning, the living area's soaring 20-foot ceiling made it difficult for the space to feel complete. "We were able to help the room feel more full by installing floor-to-ceiling drapery panels," Emily notes. "But to keep your eye focused on the lower portion of the room, we detailed approximately 40 inches of the panels with a fun zebra print."

"I would have to say that my design philosophy would be to complete each room 110 percent before moving on to the next. Stay true to your style, even if that makes your home different from everyone else's." — EMILY HEWETT

"What makes a design 'Southern' to us is a sophisticated color palette paired with little details such as embellishments or embroidered monograms," says Emily. She adds that she has a penchant for designing serene bedrooms. This polished master's sanctuary boasts characteristic icy-blue hues sure to inspire the sweetest of dreams.

living in
HARMONY

Price and Joy Kloess's home was lovely—but too busy—thus Joy began a design overhaul. "The house looked too choppy with red dining-room walls, a yellow den and kitchen, and a striped two-tone foyer. Plus, I had art and mirrors on every wall," she recalls. "I wanted the rooms to flow together harmoniously." Once the downstairs was repainted, Joy admits she was hesitant to hang anything. "It was so much more restful on the eye to let the color, along with the drapes, some good art, and antiques, grab the spotlight and not have the busyness of filling all four walls with décor." Now, warm tones flow seamlessly from the entrance to the adjoining rooms and provide a perfect backdrop for the impressive array of antiques and objets d'art found within. The circa-1940s zebra rug, for instance, came from an estate of a Palm Beach doctor, while a number of large abstract paintings are the work of a local Alabama painter. Antiques, of course, steal the show in the Kloess abode. Priceless treasures dating back to the 1700s hail from France and Belgium and include rich, sumptuous fabrics. Artfully combining all these elements, Joy stays true to her palette. "Keeping things neutral not only gives you a calmer, fluid feel, but it doesn't scream midcentury modern or country French or English fussy or minimalistic," she promises. "The timeless look will never grow old."

A fireplace is a natural focal point, and it's especially so in the Kloess den. Here, a limestone mantel was fashioned after one Joy Kloess found in a favorite magazine, while a large abstract painting carries the eye up. The iron coffee table is the work of an area blacksmith who combined two iron balconies from France to create the conversation piece. Since the family's den and kitchen connect, Joy chose the same wall paint for both rooms. And on the windows, a dark-brown gloss works wonders on the mullions. "The glass dividers disappear as you look outside," she explains, especially at night when light-colored trim would be distracting.

LEFT: A subtle botanical theme—seen in both wall hangings and the repetition of green accents—unifies the spaces. These prints were found at an antiques shop, then custom framed locally. The buffet below them is from France.

ABOVE: Greeting guests in the foyer, this needlepoint armchair dates back to the late 1700s and is a prize possession for the family.

RIGHT: Under a grand iron chandelier from Belgium, the dining room table is solid limestone on an iron scrolled base. Joy completes the room with draperies that match her wall color, a look that is both timeless and space enhancing, she says.

"To follow any of the latest design trends, simply change out a few lamps, pillows, and maybe an occasional table. A room with an eclectic mix of furnishings is 10 times more interesting than a cookie-cutter, mass-produced theme room." — JOY KLOESS

Originally stark white, the kitchen now carries a more soothing palette with khaki cabinets and honed travertine countertops. At its center, a pine island becomes a grand gathering spot, while smart accents like bronze pendant lights and antique lace curtains give the room a polished appeal.

classical
RENDITION

Both a sense of grandeur and a feeling of familial warmth pervade this home in Alabama's capital city of Montgomery. The homeowners wanted their newly built dwelling to exude the character of time, so architect Jim Barganier and designers Judy Kyser and Jean Anderson opted for Old-World elements like exposed-brick floors, walls, and columns, and for the downstairs ceilings, salvaged wood beams that are at once dramatic and inviting. Featuring a Louisiana Lowcountry–style structure, the home's entrance includes several sets of double doors across the front portico that can be opened to the foyer to take advantage of natural light and Southern cross breezes. From the portrait above the entryway staircase to the many personal furnishings throughout, it is clear that this place is not just a dwelling but also a celebration of family. A long main hallway—which leads past several bedrooms and ends in the grandchildren's playroom—displays a cherished collection of walking canes as well as the "family album." Sepia-toned and black-and-white photographs of generations fill the wall, each one marked with a brief description in cursive. Multiple porches and balconies offer views of the beautiful garden designed by James T. Farmer III and create an easy flow to the outdoors, promising additional space for entertaining and all-important family gatherings.

Sets of doors on either side of the mantel in the living room appear to be ordinary closets, but in fact conceal shallow shelves arranged with Christmas collectibles. They open in November to reveal instant holiday trimmings.

A furnished veranda, accessible by French doors from the living room and the hallway, acts as a year-round entertaining space. Enclosed by exterior walls on three sides, the area feels intimate, but drawn curtains on the fourth wall offer an unobstructed view of the backyard garden beds, which spill with hydrangeas and other flowers for cutting.

In the guest room, the designers worked with the homeowners to choose floral motifs against a backdrop of pleasing sky blue to compose a retreat of absolute serenity. A visual contrast to the primarily bold palettes of other rooms throughout the house, the suite's design is just right for welcoming overnight visitors, and the subtle palette allows some of the ornate and antique accessories to take center stage.

"You have to make a plan. Then let that plan be your North Star in that it's always keeping you on path, but leave room for inspiration to bloom."

— JAMES T. FARMER III

Instead of a fence, a screen of Southern-favorite magnolias offers privacy from the next-door neighbors. A cottage-style gate, designed to match the shutters, adds charm to the backyard oasis. "Design is all about the relationship between functionality and beauty," says landscape designer James T. Farmer III.

James created the
raised flower beds to be
wheelchair accessible and then
filled them with fragrant herbs,
textured plants, and flowers for
cutting that are within easy reach.

cultivated ELEGANCE

Well-designed interiors start with visions of luxurious fabrics, fetching antiques, original art, fine furniture, and—if you're Anita Rankin—homeowners kicking off their shoes and fully enjoying every inch of their redesigned home. "It's my responsibility to help clients create the house or the room that they want to live in," says Anita. And by "live," she truly means *live*. The idea is no more evident than in Anita's own home in Fairhope, Alabama, where she thinks nothing of walking over the antique rugs on her bathroom floor, stacking dishes in a grand armoire, and serving meals in her "formal" dining room for ordinary occasions. "I live all over it," says the 30-year veteran designer, who simply doesn't believe in rooms or furnishings that aren't enjoyed everyday and by everyone. "My grandchildren, my dog, and my granddog live on every piece of furniture in this house," she promises. Anita designed her own dining room to be versatile; the elegant but laid-back setting suits both quiet evening meals and grand dinner parties. She chose a table that expands to seat from 6 to 16 and surrounded it with chic mix-and-match chairs. A closer look at the space reveals some savvy spots here and there in the form of leopard print, and gilded details appear in various ways from ceiling to floor. Though the look is refined, opulent, and altogether exquisite, the atmosphere remains warm and approachable, much like the designer herself. Indeed, she has mastered the art of living well.

Use every room in the house—that's one of designer Anita Rankin's cardinal rules. She says, "Turn rooms into spaces you want to use." For large, bare walls, she notes a huge painting is a nice option but also suggests that an attractive screen used as a wall hanging will provide the same effect for less money.

"The secret to designing a well-loved and well-lived-in home is found in understanding that the house and all of its accents and elements should suit the personality and the lifestyle of the people who plan to dwell there." — ANITA RANKIN

Anita's dining room features classic pieces with Old-World charm and accents with sass and class. "Your space should suit you," she says, smiling, "and your lifestyle." Take the dining room, for example: "If you're not going to use it because it's formal, don't do it formal," says the designer. She recalls a client who said she couldn't wait to have Christmas dinner in her "incredible" new dining room. Anita gasped, "Christmas dinner?! What about tonight?"

"I really love to do powder rooms up big," says Anita. Antique chairs, oil paintings, hand-painted wallpaper, and many other fine accents find their way into these tiny spaces. She also treats the kitchen as if it were any other room. An iron chandelier hangs above the island, curtains line the cabinet doors, and an armoire, not a cupboard, holds Anita's fine china. "You spend a lot of time in your kitchen and your bathroom," she points out. "Why not put beautiful things in there?"

The Rankins' master suite is a haven as well as a memory gallery, filled with family pictures and unique finds from many travels. French doors open to the back porch and sounds from the bay. Sweet music on stringed instruments also permeates the air here as both Anita and her husband play and sing—and King Charles Spaniel Sophie basks in every moment of it.

artistic
IMPRESSION

With two active children and one on the way, Brent and Christen Bensten seized the opportunity to fulfill their dream of building a home together. "We realized we were going to officially outgrow our one-story rambler, and it was time," says Christen. Brent's construction background and her design acumen both came into play to complete the project, which presented the challenge of meeting their large family's needs on one of the small lots in Arlington, Virginia, outside of Washington, D.C. "We wanted to design a house that was spacious but offered many cozy areas for our family and friends to gather comfortably." For the downstairs level, they settled on an open-concept plan that would create an easy flow for entertaining and also help keep the children in sight. For architectural details and the interior design, Christen drew on the cottage style that always enchanted her while reading Jane Austen and Charlotte Brontë novels during her childhood. "I wanted window seats, balconies, and pitched-roof lines to mirror country English homes," she says. The project also unwittingly launched Christen's popular blog and business, Blue Egg Brown Nest, which features furnishings refinished in Chalk Paint decorative paint by Annie Sloan. "We had no budget for furniture, so I had to get creative," she says. "The painted pieces in my home were refinished with my own hands, and I am very proud of that."

ABOVE: Even the front door and the porch of the Benstens' two-story cedar echo Christen Bensten's thoughts on Southern style. "I love the idea of creating warmth and a welcoming atmosphere. I want people to feel comfortable in my home and not like they have to tiptoe around my furnishings." LEFT: A handsome grandfather clock, bird nests in cloches, and framed music scores are just a few of the details found in the sitting room off the entry. Says Christen, "I love that on every surface is at least one vintage accent that gives my home a look of unique interest."

Christen discovered this antique library card catalog at a barn sale and decided it would be perfect as an unexpected sideboard in her dining room. She says, "I think there needs to be a mix of elements in a space to make it work and not look too monotonous."

In the living room, three sets of
French doors lead to a Juliet
balcony, adding an air of romance.
Custom-designed, hinged panels
of framed art hide the television.

Open to the living room and an informal dining space—which features the French wheat-back chairs that were Christen's first-ever project—the kitchen follows the same philosophy as the rest of the house, with personality added through accents and textiles.

"When I think of Southern style, I think of a warm, hospitable space that is welcoming to friends and neighbors. It is a home that is bright, breezy, and comfortable with effortless elegance." — CHRISTEN BENSTEN

Estate sales have been the source for many of the curiosities and statement pieces in Christen's interiors, such as this mustard antique velvet chair that rests near a long window seat in the casual dining area. She explains, "I think mixing old and new is really key in getting a space to look like you spent a lot of money on your design."

"I create a rustic yet polished look with touches of vintage items alongside new upholstery and case goods. For example, wooden dough bowls, old bird cages, and candlesticks look great next to silk curtains and pillows with pom-poms." Christen also considers her interests when choosing accents—stacks of antique books are piled on nearly every surface, and a vintage typewriter in her office nods to her love of writing.

Believing a bedroom should be a "calm respite," Christen designed the master bedroom with a slightly different feel than the rest of the house, relying on multiple layers of creamy fabrics to compose a heavenly retreat. Personal mementos and rustic accessories, such as shutters that can serve as a room divider, bring dimension to the room.

farmhouse
HEART & SOUL

Shea Halliburton Wright's first three years of life were spent in a 1920s guesthouse on her family's 80-acre farm in Clarksville, Tennessee. For three generations, this tiny abode has been much more than a starter home for the newlyweds in the family. Rather, the cozy cottage is symbolic of new beginnings—an experience Shea had firsthand when she moved back to the family farm in 2010. Her initial design challenge was to make 900 square feet seem more spacious. Shea and her father began with the ceiling, unveiling original beams under old drywall. Coats of white paint on the ceiling and walls created a blank canvas, instant airiness, and a striking contrast to the dyed ebony floors. In the kitchen, quick cosmetic changes produced dramatic results. Sticking with a monochromatic color scheme, Shea enlisted her family to craft concrete countertops, paint cabinets, and give walls a Venetian faux finish. From there, decorating began. "I love mixing modern, clean lines with paint-chipped antiques to create an unexpected look," Shea explains. For example: In the dining room, she paired Lucite chairs with a large oak table. "I knew clear chairs wouldn't take up much visual space, allowing this open-concept area to appear less cluttered." When Shea married Josh in 2012, the two combined their creativity, filling the rooms with personalized art, which they requested in lieu of traditional wedding gifts. Overall, the chic floor-to-ceiling makeover has given this treasured Tennessee farmhouse new life—and new love.

The Wrights' handsome whippet, Jenkins, loves to lounge in the sunlight—especially on his favorite blanket in the living room. Here, a modern gray sectional pairs with an old golden chair, while a worn trunk doubles as both storage and a coffee table. Anchoring the space is a graphic charcoal rug, which breaks up the neutrals of the room with a bold pattern.

ABOVE LEFT & OPPOSITE: In the kitchen, Shea Halliburton Wright's brother-in-law poured concrete countertops to replace her damaged Formica ones. Says Shea, "I wanted a monochromatic kitchen that integrated different materials and textures." User-friendly concrete is temperature hearty and has proven easy to maintain as well.

ABOVE RIGHT: The letter *S* appears in all sizes on a bathroom wall, while antique cameras can be spotted on tables and shelves throughout the house—a nod to Shea's career as a photographer. To achieve a similar look, she suggests the following: "Keep collections looking curated, not cluttered, by purchasing only items you truly love."

"We'll always look fondly on our time here in the little house. There's just something so special about coming back to where you started." — SHEA HALLIBURTON WRIGHT

In the master bedroom, a restored iron bed is accompanied by mismatched nightstands— on the left, a dental chest and on the right, a modern cubby. Nearly 30 years after Shea came home here as an infant, her cottage has become a newlywed haven. She and her architect husband may have grand visions for their abode, but one thing remains certain: You *can* go home again.

everything is
ILLUMINATED

This 1920s Spanish Revival has plenty of stories to tell. The latest, though, is most certainly its brightest. "From the exterior, it had a timeless charm and elegance, sitting above the street on a gently sloping lot, with a backdrop of beautiful trees," says homeowner Leigh Ferrell. "The interior was a different story. There were charming features, but elements from the original floor plan and finishes needed updating for this lovely house to become a home that worked for a busy family." Leigh employed full-service firm Christopher Architecture & Interiors and designer Joanna Goodman. "We were asked to update the dark and uninviting interiors while being respectful of its history," Joanna explains. "By repainting all the rooms neutral colors and replacing the heavy window treatments with light linens, the house instantly was brighter and full of light. We studied the floor plan and created a better circulation pattern, straightened out awkward angles, and gained storage areas in the process." And then there was light! The new, more functional floor plan maximized the light coming into the house from the existing French doors and windows. "What had been a choppy, somewhat dark interior became a beautiful light-filled space." Thanks to a wonderful synergy with her design team, Leigh says her home can finally reflect her family's personality—light, bright, and most definitely welcoming.

Maintaining and enhancing the original character of the house was key for the builders and designer Joanna Goodman. The team restored the original fireplace, replicated the 12-inch plaster crown moldings, maintained the original Spanish tile, and matched existing door hardware with new. "The result is a house full of light, period details, and a thoughtful material palette. What couldn't be salvaged was re-created," Joanna adds. Ample seating was chosen in family-friendly, comfortable fabrics for guests to gather. Plus, in the breakfast room (above), a custom banquette makes morning-time meals—or impromptu entertaining—a cinch.

"Complementing the original character of the house, we custom-designed lighting, the zinc hood, and a banquette in the kitchen," says Joanna. There's also new perspective: You can see into the rest of the first floor living spaces, as well as out into the front and side yards, all from the kitchen.

The master suite previously added to the home had a number of awkward angles, a concrete floor, and dark finishes. Now shades of cream, white, silver, and gold dance around the serene space. Says homeowner Leigh Farrell, "The master bedroom is beautiful and calm, with clean lines, and it finally feels like part of the original house rather than an afterthought."

"My wish has always been to have a beautiful, comfortable home for my children, filled with love. It's not about cost or space, but rather about the care, thought, and love you put into the space."

— LEIGH FARRELL

Thanks to the addition of a pedestal tub, improved lighting, and stunning marble tile, the renovation resulted in a new master bathroom reminiscent of a high-end spa. "This space seems like my own wonderful light-filled retreat," notes homeowner Leigh Farrell. Simple matted sketches and mirrored frames add easy interest to the walls without introducing distracting hues.

One particularly beautiful result of the family's home renovation was newfound storage solutions. "A place for everything and everything in its place," recites Leigh. In this sunny office area, classic built-in bookcases leave plenty of room for a colorful library. Some people sort their volumes by theme, but in this abode, color coordination reveals a cheerful contrast to the white shelves and desk. "Every room in this house was so much improved by either the structural redesign or the beautiful finishes and interiors, that my favorite is whichever room I am in at the time!" Leigh says. "But mostly I love the way the house works for my family and me."

rustic
REDEFINED

Polished and inviting, elegant and livable—when the Colliers set about decorating their home, they wanted a space with style that was still family friendly. With basketball games and tennis matches mixed into the family's busy schedule, they also needed room to comfortably entertain whole teams of teenagers. "They wanted to use all of the living spaces—no velvet ropes allowed," explains Fran Keenan, the Deep South designer with whom the Colliers worked to achieve their vision. The home already had good bones and well-proportioned rooms, so Fran helped the family build on that solid foundation, updating and adding more personality where needed. Selecting a fresh palette of grays, blues, and white, they used the family's collection of antique pieces to complement the décor and add warmth. Likewise in the kitchen, they installed antique accents, which softened a state-of-the-art space that could easily accommodate large gatherings. The natural gray tones of centuries-old salvaged wood helped drive the color and overall aesthetic of the design, setting a tone of relaxed refinement. The result was the kind of home Fran imagines the family enjoying together for years to come. "It was thrilling to strike that balance of stylish yet still extremely comfortable," she relates. "The house feels warm and stylish but welcomes relaxation."

An Indian floral print on the drapery fabric, with its array of blues and grays, inspired the overall color scheme of the living room. Designer Fran Keenan accented the choice hues with soft, comfortable furniture that allowed the family to easily relax together. The room's real showpiece became the tray ceiling, which they clad in oak wood skins. Fran says, "This enabled us to make the room more casual, added lots of style, and provided unbelievable warmth to the feel of the space."

"I believe that comfort and beauty can and do coexist in the best homes. I also believe that your house should work for you, not make life harder. The best homes are layered and should reflect the personalities and interests of their owners."

— FRAN KEENAN

A palette of grays, blues, and warm brown accents drove the living room décor—a color scheme that Fran carried through to the entryway. The rich browns of the family's antiques served as the perfect complement to the elements she added to the space, and the blend of old and new resulted in an updated look that still felt pleasantly livable.

Designing a functional yet stylish kitchen was high on the Collier family's wish list. "They wanted something timeless and crisp but with antique details for added warmth," Fran explains. A pair of antique French shuttered doors anchored the design, creating an element that was simultaneously refined and casual. Their aged look matched the custom vent hood, which gave the space added historical feel. With those pieces in place, the dine-in, open-concept design left ample room for friends and family to enjoy a meal together. "Antiques and vintage items bring soul to a home like nothing else," says Fran. "An artful mix of old and new things can be the best way to give your décor longevity."

The bathrooms were designed to provide a relaxing refuge from the busyness of everyday life. With marble walls and pale-gray tile floors, the light interior set a soothing tone. For a retreat-style feel, the room includes a luxury shower stall and romantic freestanding bathtub, while vintage-inspired hardware complements the décor of the rest of the home. No need for large embellishments that would upset the tranquility of this special space—a small bouquet of fresh flowers in a bold color offers nature's joyful finishing touch.

"Sometimes beauty can be intimidating, so I enjoyed finding ways to keep the beautiful rooms still approachable; otherwise, they don't get used," Fran says. The master bedroom carried through the home's balance of style and comfort, with a tapestry and brown toile pillows lending refined polish to a space that also pleasantly housed bedside books and framed family photos.

the comforts
OF HOME

With two young children and a love of entertaining, the Pearson family needed a house that worked hard. New to Texas, but well acquainted with fine design, they chose the firm A Well Dressed Home to ensure their Dallas tudor would reflect the Southern style they loved. "What inspired us the most was the home itself—it exudes a traditional charm that we knew we wanted to carry throughout," say designers Emily Hewett and Allison Walker. The team began by neutralizing the living room, choosing light, bright tones to contrast the original hardwoods and play up the stained-glass windows. Plenty of seating in family-friendly fabrics ensured the room would stand the test of time—and football-watching parties. As with most early 20th-century homes, the challenge was how to best outfit its smaller-scale spaces. At approximately 9 feet by 8 feet, the Pearsons' daughter's room required smart storage solutions that still had darling details. Their son's room, meanwhile, was anchored by twin beds and a color scheme he could grow up with. Emily says a favorite element of the tudor was in the family's home office: "The metallic gold–painted ceiling tiles are so unexpected—and so fun!" Yet it was the homeowner herself who perhaps made the biggest impact. "Mrs. Pearson is Southern and sophisticated—characteristics we strive to incorporate in all our designs."

The Pearsons needed ample, durable seating for their high-traffic living room, but they also wanted the designers' signature light, bright fabrics. Neutral tones enhanced the room, while custom pillows and pops of black and brass added perfect doses of preppy and modern style.

LEFT: Located just off the entry, the Pearsons' office needed to be tailored yet fully functional. The design team selected a metallic paint for the detailed tin ceiling and applied a fresh coat of white to the brick walls. A credenza behind the desk houses electronics and files, while a simple white bookcase holds keepsakes and framed pictures.

ABOVE & OPPOSITE: The living room's neutral color palette lets the stunning stained-glass windows steal the show, while a geometric ottoman lends a modern touch to the design.

"I would have to say the kids' rooms were my favorite part of this project. It was so much fun to introduce them to their new spaces, decked out with fresh colors and fun fabrics that were sophisticated, not stuffy." — EMILY HEWETT

Designers Emily Hewett and Allison Walker embraced the challenge of this dainty little girl's space by placing the full-size bed in the center of the back wall and flanking it with nightstands that were large enough to store books and toys. A monogrammed headboard, pink pom-pom drum shades, and a ruffled bedskirt completed the cute look.

The pair designed this handsome little boy's room around antique twin beds passed down through the family. Crisp white and bold navy made a perfect palette—carried from the bead-board walls to the striking ceiling. An industrial iron and rope light fixture, plus a navy, white, and gold campaign dresser, added elements of sophistication, while a school desk and a world map created a well-appointed place to study.

eclectic &
EXQUISITE

When stylist, interior designer, and California girl Dayka Robinson bought her charming fixer-upper

in Stone Mountain, Georgia, she was excited to have an opportunity to create a home that completely

reflected her own sensibility. "I'm a fun and fabulous single woman with no kids, so my home is really

my castle in which I can do what I please with no dissenting opinions," she says. In a style she describes

as "eclectic traditional," the look is built on a foundation of classic lines accented by unexpected pattern

and vintage whimsy. "While I love working with color—and I encourage my clients to do so—I realized

I am happiest with a timeless black, white, brown, and gold color scheme," she says. After establishing

a backdrop of bold, graphic wallpapers and patterns, Dayka set about filling her home with uniquely

charming pieces. Inspired by her abiding affection for retro furniture and accessories, she scoured

vintage shops, flea markets, and antiques stores to achieve her collected look. "When it comes to

hardware and detailing," she notes, "you just can't beat the details on vintage finds." From the smallest

accent to the big vision, Dayka's projects line up with her life philosophy: Live with intention. She says,

"I think it's paramount to just *be* in your space for a while to figure out how you really want to live

before tackling any design plan. Think about your needs, your wants, and how you can best make your

home support the highest vision of your lifestyle; then design around that."

"The best homes are not necessarily the ones with the most eye-catching décor but the ones that support homeowners leading the lives they really want to live. Have the courage to break the rules, and design your home for the life you want, not just the life you have now." —DAYKA ROBINSON

When designer Dayka Robinson moved to the South, she was determined to keep her brand-new oversize furniture, but the home's smaller footprint posed a decorating challenge. She says, "Once I decided to stop fighting against the space that I had and go with the flow—meaning waiting to find the right pieces that really worked for how I wanted to use my space—everything came together."

"Because I intentionally wanted to fill my home with secondhand pieces, I let the furniture dictate the vision," says Dayka. "Each time I found a piece I loved—the oversize vintage table lamps, vintage Brass sputnik chandelier, the pair of James Mont–style occasional chairs—the vision became clearer and clearer."

"I won't throw a party without sending paper invitations in the mail and a thank-you card to follow up after my event," says Dayka, an entertaining expert. One of her secrets for success is a refinished bar cart that works as a drink station or an additional serving space.

the color of
WONDERFUL

A heart of hospitality and a head for ingenuity have long been decorator Melissa Salem's tools for designing dream homes. When she and her husband decided to relocate from Birmingham's suburbs to the countryside with their two teenage children, the move offered an opportunity for her to use those gifts in the most personal of ways. Her vision was simple: Make a home where everybody feels welcome. "We wanted a place of refuge not just for us but for the people in our lives," she says. Inspired by a rural upbringing, she wanted the new home to mimic the feeling of the house where she was raised. "It was very warm and full of a lot of family and cooking, and everything centered around the kitchen," she says. "When I met my builder, Kevin Kennemer, I knew I'd finally met someone who could make in three dimensions what I saw in my head." Although the structure is large, Melissa says the couple was on a budget to execute her vision. "I have the old champagne taste," she jokes. Tales of finding second-hand décor elements everywhere from antiques shops to the side of the road follow. She adds, "I want my home and the other houses I design to feel collected rather than bought." From room to room, color wanders and eye-catching curiosities show up in interesting ways. "I love surprises in design," says Melissa, "and unexpected texture and pops of color are good ways to do this." All around, marvels abound, sparking stories and conversations that only add to the unique atmosphere.

For a quick update, designer Melissa Salem suggests the following: "Splurge on some fabulous textured fabric for new den pillows; wallpaper a ceiling in an unexpected pattern; paint a small room high gloss; and be sure scale of pattern is in check. Your wallpapers or fabrics should adjust to the scale of the room itself."

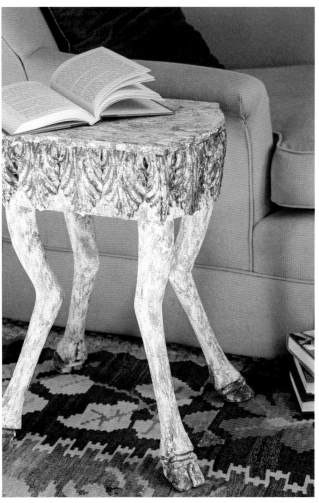

From family photos of generations past to collected works of art from around the globe, treasures in the Salem home come in many forms and fashions, including a curious hoof-foot table (above right). Melissa says, "My design is always based on good lines. It's never trendy, but perhaps it's a little quirky. Never buy something just because it's the trend. Good design should endure. I think a home should have a mix of contemporary and antiques to create interest. It's a balancing act."

Living color is a theme repeated throughout this alluring abode, and in Melissa's spacious kitchen, it is expressed in quite captivating ways. Iridescent glass mosaic tile shines as the background for a built-in bookcase, and a copper hood, treated to reflect the appearance of an oxidized patina, lends timeless European appeal to the space. The large, custom island—also in a faux finish—was designed specifically for entertaining. "We wanted a home where people felt at ease, and we wanted a home that we could share with other people and where we could have fund-raisers for ministries," Melissa says. "I wanted it to be a home and not just a museum or some kind of decorator show house."

In a mix of bold hues and brilliant patterns, luxe fabrics turn the bedroom into a refreshing escape. Neutrals provide the backdrop, while flowers and plants make the look verdant and vibrant.

"A Southern home does not have to be big in scale but rather big in heart and love and community. A Southern home says you are more important than my to-do list. It's about caring for one another in genuine ways." — MELISSA SALEM

"I believe our homes should tell our stories and journeys," says Melissa, who treats entryways as a sort of "style sneak peek" of what's to come. "When I find pieces that speak to me, I buy them and always find a way to fit them in. These special finds are what make a house a home. I don't buy to impress; I buy what I love and whatever adds joy and color and story."

nautical
GETAWAY

When Chuck and Lauren Welden purchased "The Cottage" in 2013, the couple envisioned a comfortable gathering spot for family and friends. The second home's proximity to sand and shore made it an ideal vacation place, but more importantly, it was only a hop and a skip from Lauren's sister, Jeramy, and her family. The three-bedroom, two-bathroom abode "lives large," the Weldens say, thanks to the conversion of a front living area into a dining room that adjoins an open kitchen. Other design choices, such as crisp, white paint and well-proportioned furnishings, made the space feel open and inviting. Although Lauren and Jeramy collectively decorated the home, Birmingham-based designer Virginia Volman led the sisters' vision, from palette and furniture to decorative accessories. A bicycle painting became a natural first art purchase once the family secured cruisers outfitted with baskets. From there, a whimsical school of fish and a large commissioned octopus made the bedrooms "electric with color," creating happy, welcoming spaces for guests. Just months into the project, Lauren and Jeramy's mother—affectionately called "Jo"—passed away unexpectedly, prompting the sisters to incorporate her memory throughout the cottage. As a result, the little home became an instrument of healing, a portrait of hope, and an idyllic haven for all the magical memories yet to be made.

By pairing the family's beloved blue with bright yellow and chartreuse accents, the living room gained a lively, sea-inspired feel. Framed fan coral and an end table with legs fashioned from sturdily bundled branches, display the decorative potential of beachside found objects. Even a vintage swimsuit becomes artwork (left); designer Virginia Volman showcased the piece in a shadowbox-style frame, mounting it to a navy grass cloth background.

"We selected a blue and white theme to reflect our mother's love for blue. We're natives of Hattiesburg, Mississippi, and in our home there, every single room offered a pop of blue either in a lamp, pillows, wallpaper, a vase, or a special frame." — LAUREN WELDEN

Armed with a vision for a unique dining table, homeowner Lauren Welden employed the talent of a local carpenter who used salvaged wood from the original Tutwiler Hotel in downtown Birmingham. She says, "The wood was not perfectly level, but much like a puzzle, he crafted a tabletop that provides a sanctuary of memorable mealtime conversations."

"With trundles as well as the larger bunk beds, a lot of sleepy heads can find rest in here," assures Lauren. No doubt, an army of wee ones delights in this creative space. Here, a coat of soft gray paint brightened old hardwood floors, while a royal-blue cowhide rug and a child's boat bed complete the nautical theme with a touch of whimsy.

lakeside
CHATEAU

For Frances and Beau Stanford, designing and building a house on Alabama's Lake Logan Martin was a project destined to become a family affair. Frances co-owns Maison de France Antiques in Leeds, Alabama, with the couple's daughter Ginny, and their other daughter, Mallory Smith, who is an accomplished interior designer. Then there's their son-in-law, Ben Smith, a skilled craftsman in his own right. From the collection of furniture Ginny and Frances began storing during regular buying trips to France to Mallory's particular eye for balancing contemporary design with fine antiques to Ben's ability to showcase the heirloom treasures—the family had each facet of the home construction and decorating process covered. "It was all about family," Frances recalls. "And it was a really positive experience." With architectural plans inspired by the French countryside to complement the European wares displayed throughout the interiors, Frances says they call the house their "petit chateau." As much as the family collaborated on the house's physical creation, it was also designed to be a place where all three of the Stanfords' children could gather with their spouses and children and comfortably enjoy themselves. With clean lines, open interiors, and a soothing color palette of warm neutrals, the finished home became something comfortable, livable, and, Frances attests, overwhelmingly happy.

"The kids have the run of the house," homeowner Frances Stanford says of the couple's eight grandchildren, who can be found playing both inside and outside. Rather than being protective of the historical items throughout the home, Frances incorporated the collection into family life. They used a buffet deux corps to tastefully house the television. Likewise, the coffee table was an old leather-covered gymnastics mat. On days when the weather keeps the grandchildren inside, Frances says they clear off the table and playfully jump from it onto the nearby knole sofas—English pieces from the turn of the 20th century. She adds, "Antiques are not hard to live with, you just need the right mind-set."

By using neutral tones in the upholstery and paint color throughout the home, designer Mallory Smith created a space where the antique furniture could add interest without crowding the interiors. The home's clean, uncomplicated rooms allowed special pieces, like this French farmhouse table, to feel warm and approachable.

With large rooms and high ceilings, the home's design included ample space throughout for showcasing favorite pieces that Frances and daughter Ginny found while perusing European vendors. A centuries-old hutch holds unique fish plates, which Frances chose specifically for the lake house. For the special details the Stanfords wanted incorporated into the home's construction, they relied on son-in-law Ben Smith to help make them happen. Frances recalls sitting on a 5-gallon drum in the kitchen when the house was under construction, while Ben "just drew the hood on the wall and then built it."

"Fine antiques make a house a home. They make it look more refined, while adding warmth."

— FRANCES STANFORD

A careful observer of historical and contemporary trends, Frances has watched a number of accent pieces go in and out of style. A favorite find, the sunburst mirror above the bed is from the 1800s. Paired with the soft bedding Mallory selected for the room, it offers an unexpected modern touch.

lowcountry GRANDEUR

When the entry gates swing open to this 10-acre estate on Bluffton, South Carolina's Colleton River, there's no doubt that the homeowners have created something special. Inspired by the brilliant chateaus of France, this Lowcountry property includes a guesthouse with a pool and spa, plus acres of majestic gardens that thrive in the Southern sunshine. Yet it's the 20,000-square-foot mansion that truly defines gentility. "The design was an accumulation of past homes we've owned, plus many ideas from our foreign—mostly European—travels, and many pictures from various magazines," say the homeowners, the Rowley family. Working with Atlanta-based architectural firm Nichols, Carter & Grant, the Rowleys spent more than a year making alterations that achieved their desired results. Indeed, the finished look is quite European, and given the stunning setting, "should be there 500 years from now," the family says. Throughout, the architectural details boast both historical and sentimental significance. The main office is paneled in a wormy chestnut recovered from a barn in East Tennessee, while leaded-glass panes in the tearoom's vaulted ceiling graced a New York hotel in the 18th century. The homeowners suggest that for this type of building, reviewing old architecture and studying the best contemporary methods are essential. The goal, they say, is timelessness. And the result at this home was style sure to remain fashionable.

This turreted entrance with stone facade boasts a commanding appearance sure to offer a warm Bluffton welcome any time of the year. Sunlight floods through curved doors wrapped in ornamental ironwork and illuminate the hand-painted silk wallpaper from China that graces the foyer walls. From here, the expansive home opens up to room after room of impeccable design, making it abundantly clear that the Rowleys attended to the design's every possible detail.

"We desired a somewhat sophisticated home of excellent quality, yet made every effort to maintain individual areas that were comfortable for just two people to relax and enjoy." —THE ROWLEYS

The family's Embassy Room is paneled with warm wood from the Hungarian Embassy in Paris, which was constructed in 1830. Hand-carved and accented with a shimmering gold leaf, the paneling even bears a telltale bullet hole acquired during World War II.

The grandeur of the dining room is accentuated by ornate details throughout. The intricate valences over the dining room windows include hand-carved accents found in Italy, and the garden-inspired wallpaper was printed by hand. The mahogany mantel was fashioned by a local craftsman, taking two years to complete. The Rowleys arranged the romantic setting with multiple round tables, each with an oft-replenished centerpiece of fresh flowers. The design allows the family to entertain with ease so that those gathered for an elegant meal might enjoy themselves in personal, face-to-face fashion.

The home's expansive master suite features three fireplaces, a sitting area, a dressing room, walk-in closets, and his and hers bathrooms. One of the most captivating elements, though, is the ornate bed, a custom, regal rococo-style piece.

signature
ITALIAN STYLE

After 17 years of idyllic Italian living, interior designer Lisa Gabrielson and her family moved to Atlanta in 2006. Here, surrounded by decidedly Southern style, Lisa set about making their new house a familiar home. "While in Italy, we collected antiques and family heirlooms—we wanted our home in Atlanta to be a fresh interpretation of the Tuscan farmhouse we used to live in," Lisa says. The main design challenge, she explains, was to take out the "cookie-cutter" aspect of suburban homes. She says, "I overcame this with the use of unique antiques and architectural elements." Lisa added chippy wooden corbels to the kitchen counter and antique French shutters to interior windows, and she hand-painted finishes on built-in bookshelves. The result: "Virtually every room in our home features personalized elements. It has been a work in progress, reflecting our history as a family and our casual yet sophisticated style," she says. The massive mural in the living room, for example, is a wedding present from her parents, depicting the Tuscan hills where they lived. "Embrace family heirlooms, but use them in an updated way. By keeping the walls white and the upholstery neutral, antique pieces look fresh and featured." Lisa defines Southern style as "casual and relaxed, with a nod to tradition, a touch of whimsy, and a big dose of class." One look at her home and there's no doubt she's fluent.

Designer Lisa Gabrielson added antique European shutters to these soaring windows to give the space extra patina and to warm up the 20-foot-tall great room.

"I home in on my clients' personal style, whether their taste is modern, traditional, transitional, or cottage. My style lies somewhere between these labels, and as a self-taught designer, I believe there are no rules in design. The bottom line for me is to create beautiful, inspiring, and above all, comfortable spaces." — LISA GABRIELSON

"Good design does not need to cost a lot," says Lisa. "Shop thrift stores and antique malls for furniture and accessories that are high on charm and easy on the wallet." In the heart of her home, for example, this charming set of painted kitchen chairs was a serendipitous yard sale score.

This iron headboard was found at an
Italian antiques market, while the layers
upon layers of sumptuous linens hail
from France, Italy, and America.

personal COLLECTION

Hal and Janice Gaultney had a very clear vision of the home they hoped to buy. Having just returned to Alabama after three years in Belgium, the two began their search in the beautiful historic districts of Huntsville. A chance meeting with a friendly couple, the Inschos, led them to nearby Decatur, where they toured a Queen Anne that would be undergoing extensive restoration. The couple loved the home but needed to settle in before the start of the school year, so they instead purchased a new home in Huntsville. Still, Janice recalls, "We couldn't let the desire for an older home go." Two years later, while reviewing real estate ads, the Gaultneys saw this headline: "Victorian Beauty Restored by Architect/Builder in Decatur." "We knew it must be the Inscho home, went to see it, and fell in love!" Then, the fun began as Hal and Janice worked to combine their vast collection of family heirlooms with functional furnishings for a busy family. This worked particularly well in the creamy and classic white kitchen, which blends with the style of the home yet has all the modern conveniences. Here, dinner is prepared and homework done side by side. "Mixing new and old pieces was a bit of a challenge, but it was a challenge I relished!" Janice adds. "I cannot paint as my husband and many friends can; my home is my canvas."

"Although we treasured the Victorian architecture of our home, we wanted the interior to be less formal, lighter, and perhaps more like the French cottages we had seen in Europe," says homeowner Janice Gaultney. "We had collected lovely blue platters, plates, and pitchers, as well as family and flea-market furniture treasures and wished to use them in our home." The resulting space was both sophisticated and casual, with comfortable furnishings amid prized keepsakes.

Whenever possible in bedrooms, Janice prefers to position the bed on the wall opposite of the main door. She says, "Your bed is the beautiful focal point of your room. Place it where you see it first!" Throughout the bedrooms in this home, the walls are painted in lighter hues, and the linens are mostly white. This provides a clean and uncomplicated canvas for showcasing antiques.

"I have always loved anything old, especially things with a story. Our mothers and grandmothers knew we wanted any item they were willing to pass on to us, and they would be pleased to see that we treasure every piece they passed along. That gives me joy." — JANICE GAULTNEY

An arched arbor and a white fence blanketed in green create a sweet scene characteristic of the home's history and Southern setting. "A Southern home should be pleasing to the eye, comfortable, and welcoming," Janice reflects. "It's so satisfying to hear guests use those words to describe our home."

outdoor
INSPIRATION

A good deal of careful collaboration went into the renovation of Margaret Taylor and Martha Johnson's Atlanta-area home. "The major themes were openness, light, welcoming, and focusing eyes on our backyard," say the homeowners. "The house needed to welcome people in a warm and casual way, whether it's a few folks for a cookout or a gaggle of friends cheering on the University of Alabama Crimson Tide during Saturday football games." To get the gears going, Margaret and Martha invited over a few couples for a brainstorming dinner. Then, they got out the paper. "We spent a lot of time drawing, sketching, and doodling ideas. How would the fireplace be more attractive and enjoyable? How will the space accommodate our dinner parties? And what would it look like if we hosted Thanksgiving?" they recall. "We are not professionals, but anyone can block out a room and put down ideas for walls, furniture, and window placement." When the time came, they did employ the professionals, including Trish Land, a designer with a keen eye for out-of-the-box style. Clever solutions include a wood and steel mantel installation that hides electronics, along with a hearth fashioned out of concrete pavers that displays succulents or ferns. Above all, Margaret and Martha suggest taking your time to let designs evolve. "Bounce ideas off your friends, and imagine what it will feel like and flow like in real life," they say—and ultimately, "trust your own instincts and aesthetics."

"We wanted our kitchen to feel like a gathering place—not only in seating, but to feel like a room. We tried to achieve this by not having any hanging cabinets and by having a table in the middle that serves several purposes around 'gathering.'"

— MARGARET TAYLOR & MARTHA JOHNSON

In the kitchen, a number of creative solutions resolved design challenges. The homeowners chose 30-inch counters, rather than the typical 24-inch, to make a wide room more user-friendly. Then, when the adjacent dining room was too small for a dinner party, they created a wider opening between the rooms so a kitchen table could be extended to fit more friends.

Blending seamlessly into each room of the home, reclaimed materials are significant—but not overpowering—design tools. The key, the homeowners say, is making each element important and noticeable. "Too much can be very masculine and unspecial." For example, in the bathroom, the juxtaposition of textured wood and an ornate rug is both daring and delightful.

"Southern style is welcoming and comfortable, and creates access to the outdoors both visually and tactilely," explain homeowners Margaret Taylor and Martha Johnson, whose outside oasis offers multiple places to gather. "The backyard is every bit as much a part of the house as the inside, and this makes the house feel so much larger for us."

home,
SWEET HOME

Cozy, comfortable, and plenty of style—this combination of elements makes Mary Ann Corte's off-the-beaten path residence a true retreat. Warm tones blend with refreshing hues while romantic prints mix with a few select patterns in a more daring panache. In both artwork and other accents, a coastal influence breezes throughout the space as a subtle reminder of this retreat's near-the-bay locale. Architect Lea Verneuille of Fairhope, Alabama, designed the home to take advantage of its beautiful lake vistas, placing the windows to allow brilliant streams of sunlight and turn the breathtaking views into focal points. Meanwhile, Mary Ann worked with designer and friend Anita Rankin in a creative collaboration to infuse the home with a high-end yet inviting style. The rooms were laid out to showcase many of the couple's treasured antiques, as well as finds from years of perusing at the area's annual arts and crafts fair. Mary Ann combined the dining and living rooms into one large space to make entertaining easy, but cleverly arranged the furniture to visually separate the spaces and create smaller, more intimate areas for conversation. Playing off the location's rich history, this family home's tasteful décor appropriately draws from the clean lines and metallic finishes of 18th-century design. The ladies focused on foundation pieces with patina to anchor the design and completed the look with modern accents, giving the abode a pleasant balance between relaxed and refined style.

ABOVE: While on a trip to Dahlonega, Georgia, the homeowners discovered an artist who does paintings on wood. They commissioned him to create a pair of sunflower-bedecked panels that perfectly—and prettily—conceal a big-screen television when it's not in use.

RIGHT: This airy home near the water has the openness of a casual California farmhouse with an upscale French flair. The comfortable and cozy sun porch adjoins the dining room and the kitchen in one large, sweeping space that is ideal for entertaining family and friends. The polished but approachable interiors help guests feel instantly at ease.

"We all need a place we can come home to, where we can find rest and solace, as well as love and laughter. It's important to really live in the spaces we call home." —ANITA RANKIN

Designer Anita Rankin answered the homeowners' request for a quiet and restful master suite tucked away from the heart of the home and filled with marvelous window light. While the room borrows from textiles and palettes seen elsewhere in the house, sumptuous white bed linens and a simple composition of furnishings support a most relaxing vibe.

An antique table in the master suite displays stacks of favorite decorating books and precious family photographs (opposite). A few steps away, the neutral-hued haven also boasts extraordinary his-and-hers bathrooms filled with luxurious French-inspired appointments, including an elegant chandelier, whitewashed cabinetry, marble counters, and mirror-mounted sconces. The piece de resistance is the freestanding tub placed before the window in the "hers" bathroom, altogether lending a lavish European-spa feel to the surroundings.

Acknowledgments

COVER
Interiors by Emily Hewett
& Allison Walker of A Well
Dressed Home
awelldressedhome.com
Photography by John O'Hagan

TRADITION OF HOSPITALITY
Pages 16-27
Interiors by Beverly Farrington
of Accents of the South
accentsofthesouth.com
Photography by Marcy Black
Simpson

SUBTLE & SOPHISTICATED
Pages 28-33
Interiors by Emily Hewett
& Allison Walker of A Well
Dressed Home
Photography by John O'Hagan

LIVING IN HARMONY
Pages 34-41
Interiors by Joy Kloess
Photography by William Dickey
Styling by Kathleen J. Whaley

CLASSICAL RENDITION
Pages 42-53
Architectural Designs by
Jim Barganier of Barganier Davis
Sims Architects Associated
bdsarch.com
Landscape Designs by
James T. Farmer III
jamesfarmer.com
Styling by Kathleen J. Whaley

CULTIVATED ELEGANCE
Pages 54-63
Interiors by Anita Rankin of
Meriwether Interiors
251.990.4068
Photography by
Marcy Black Simpson
Styling by Andrea Fanning
& Adrienne A. Williams

ARTISTIC IMPRESSION
Pages 64-79
Interiors by Christen Bensten
of Blue Egg Brown Nest
blueeggbrownnest.com
Photography by
Stephen DeVries
Styling by Andrea Fanning

FARMHOUSE HEART & SOUL
Pages 80-87
Photography & Styling by
Shea Halliburton Wright
byshea.com

EVERYTHING IS ILLUMINATED
Pages 88-99
Interiors by Joanna Goodman
of Christopher Architecture &
Interiors
christopherai.com
Photography by
Marcy Black Simpson

RUSTIC REDEFINED
Pages 100-111
Interiors by Fran Keenan
205.821.8183

THE COMFORTS OF HOME
Pages 112-121
Interiors by Emily Hewett
& Allison Walker of A Well
Dressed Home
Photography by John O'Hagan

ECLECTIC & EXQUISITE
Pages 122-129
Interiors by Dayka Robinson of
Dayka Robinson Designs
daykarobinsondesigns.com
Photography by
Stephanie Welbourne
Styling by K. Faith Morgan

THE COLOR OF WONDERFUL
Pages 130-141
Interiors by Melissa Salem
Photography by
Stephanie Welbourne
Styling by Tracey MacMillan
Runnion

NAUTICAL GETAWAY
Pages 142-151
Interiors by Virginia Volman
Photography by William Dickey
Styling by Tracey MacMillan
Runnion

LAKESIDE CHATEAU
Pages 152-161
Interiors by Mallory Smith
mallorysmithinteriors.com
Photography by Mac Jamieson
Styling by Andrea Fanning
& Adrienne A. Williams

LOWCOUNTRY GRANDEUR
Pages 162-171
Photography by John O'Hagan

SIGNATURE ITALIAN STYLE
Pages 172-179
Interiors by Lisa Gabrielson of
Lisa Gabrielson Interior Design
lisagabrielson.com
Photography by Mac Jamieson

PERSONAL COLLECTION
Pages 180-189
Interiors by Janice Gaultney
Photography by
Kimberly Finkel Davis
Styling by Adrienne A. Williams

OUTDOOR INSPIRATION
Pages 190-197
Interiors by Trish Land
trishland.com
Photography by John O'Hagan

HOME, SWEET HOME
Pages 198-205
Interiors by Anita Rankin of
Meriwether Interiors
Styling by Andrea Fanning

Text by Andrea Fanning,
Kathleen J. Whaley, Annalise
DeVries, Lauren Eberle, K. Faith
Morgan, & Karen Callaway

To all those who had a hand in helping with this compilation, from designers and homeowners to family and friends, and to my Lord and Savior who has bestowed blessings abundant—thank you. Life is more beautiful because of you. — A. FANNING

"Every house where love abides
And friendship is a guest,
Is surely home, and home sweet home
For there the heart can rest."

— HENRY VAN DYKE